W9-CHR-834

Laura Bush

by Jill C. Wheeler

visit us at
www.abdopub.com

Published by ABDO & Daughters, an imprint of ABDO
Publishing Company, 4940 Viking Drive, Suite 622, Edina,
Minnesota 55435. Copyright ©2003 by Abdo Consulting
Group, Inc. International copyrights reserved in all countries.
No part of this book may be reproduced in any form without
written permission from the publisher.

Printed in the United States.

Edited by Paul Joseph
Graphic Design: John Hamilton
Cover Design: Mighty Media
Interior Photos: AP/Photo, p. 1, 5, 6, 9, 11, 12, 15, 16, 19, 21,
22, 28, 31, 33, 34, 36, 39, 40, 42, 45, 47, 49, 51, 52, 55, 57, 58,
60, 61
Corbis, p. 25, 26, 27

Library of Congress Cataloging-in-Publication Data

Wheeler, Jill C., 1964-
    Laura Bush / Jill C. Wheeler.
        p. cm. — (Breaking barriers)
    Includes index.
    Summary: A brief biography of the former Texas librarian and
teacher who, as the wife of the forty-third president, became first lady
in 2001.
    ISBN 1-57765-875-2
    1. Bush, Laura Welch, 1946- —Juvenile literature. 2. Presidents'
spouses—United States—Biography—Juvenile literature. [1. Bush,
Laura Welch, 1946- 2. First ladies.] I. Title.

E904.B87 W48 2002
973.931'092—dc21
[B]

2002016331

Contents

Welcome to the Family

*T*he Bush family has been a household name in American politics for many years. From stern Senator Prescott Bush to former President George H. W. Bush, the family has spent decades in the national spotlight.

The Bush family is incredibly close and loyal. They also can be loud, strict, boisterous, and fun loving. It was into that very atmosphere that an introverted librarian first walked in the fall of 1977.

Laura Welch of Midland, Texas, had just become engaged to George W. Bush. Raised as an only child, she was accustomed to a quiet house. Now she had been thrust into the middle of the rowdy Bush clan. The Bushes, meanwhile, were watching her closely. George had dated many women, but he rarely was serious about any of them. His family was curious about this new woman who had captured his heart.

President George W. Bush and First Lady Laura Bush.

Laura Bush reads to a group of children at a school library.

Among the first to scrutinize Laura was George's grandmother, Dorothy Walker Bush. The stern, steely matriarch regarded Laura coolly. "What do you do?" she asked with a wilting stare. Laura looked her straight in the eye and replied calmly, "I read."

Laura held her own with the Bushes that day. She has been holding her own ever since. A former first lady of Texas and now the first lady of the United States, the former teacher and librarian brings calmness and sincerity to all she does.

Those close to Laura say her calmness is the perfect balance to her husband's enthusiasm. Former President George H. W. Bush sums it up well. "Golly," he said, "she sure can calm him down."

Adds President George W. Bush, "She is a loving, strong, and calm lady with a wonderful smile, which reflects a kind heart."

"Most people don't know anything about me, but based on the things that have been published, people probably think I'm a shy librarian," Laura Bush said. "Well, very few librarians fit the stereotype: They're people who like knowledge and are interested in a lot of different things." And so, it would seem, is Laura Bush.

A Nice, Quiet Kiddo

*L*aura Welch was born on November 4, 1946, in Midland, Texas. She was the only child of Harold and Jenna Welch. Harold worked as a credit officer for a while. Then he took advantage of Midland's building boom in the 1950s and 1960s and he began working as a developer and home builder. Jenna became the bookkeeper for Harold's construction business. She was also active in many Midland civic clubs.

Jenna Welch recalls her daughter's childhood as quiet. "She was just born a nice quiet little kiddo," Jenna Welch said. "She was an easy baby. She never cried; she never even was sick, hardly." Laura remembers being "slightly lonely." Because her parents could not have any more children after she was born, Laura was an only child.

While she was growing up, Laura spent a lot of time simply reading. "I loved to read," she said. "My mother read to me, and I think most people who love to read, or writers, had parents who loved to read. I remember my mother calling to say, 'Come set the table,' or come do something, and I couldn't put my book down; I had to keep reading."

Laura Bush

By the time she was in second grade, Laura knew she wanted to be a teacher. A well-behaved, orderly child, she loved to play teacher while pretending that her dolls were her students. "Neither of my parents graduated from college," she recalled. "But I knew at an early age that they had high hopes and high expectations for me. My dad bought an education policy, and he always said, 'Don't worry, your education will be taken care of.'"

Laura was an A student. Her friends remember her as being more grown-up than most girls her age. She was active in Girl Scouts and in the local First Methodist Church. "In a lot of ways I had a perfect childhood," she said. "We felt very free to do whatever we wanted. You could ride your bike downtown, go to the Rexall Drug and get a ham sandwich for lunch. But at the same time, we were sheltered."

Laura's childhood wasn't always perfect, however. The year before college, Laura experienced tragedy firsthand. On a November night in 1963, 17-year-old Laura was driving through Midland when she ran a stop sign and hit another car. Her close friend, high school track star Mike Douglas, was driving the other car.

Mike died of a broken neck at the scene of the accident. Laura was not charged with a crime, but the accident devastated her and the people of Midland. It took Laura years to accept what had happened. "It was just a terrible accident that I had to come to terms with," she said later. "I didn't have a choice."

Laura Bush

Following high school, Laura enrolled at Southern Methodist University (SMU) in University Park, a suburb of Dallas, Texas. Laura joined the Kappa Alpha Theta sorority and was a popular student at SMU. Friends recalled that she usually had a boyfriend. She brought several of them back to Midland to meet her parents, yet she was never very serious about any of them.

Her parents recalled her as being well behaved at college, even though the times were turbulent for many young people. "She would never have done any protesting, or all that other '70s stuff," said a close friend.

"My generation was just right on the cusp," Laura added. "When I started at SMU, girls still wore dresses to school the whole time. I entered in 1964. It was a fairly conservative campus compared with how it was just a few years after that for the little brothers and sisters of my friends."

College to Classroom

*L*aura's friends recalled that in college she spent a lot of time reading books, magazines, and newspapers. Laura's mother, who had read to her "from the time she could open her eyes," was not surprised. Laura was usually content to let other people lead the conversation while she sat back and listened. Laura listened well, and she would amaze her friends by remembering something from a long-ago conversation as if it had happened the day before.

As in high school, Laura earned good grades in college. She graduated from SMU in 1968 with a bachelor's degree in education. Laura took time off after graduating to travel through Europe, then took a job teaching at Longfellow Elementary School in Dallas. "Many of my second, third, and fourth grade students couldn't read," she recalled of her teaching days during a speech at the 2000 Republican National Convention. "And frankly, I'm not sure I was very good at teaching them. I tried to make it fun by making the characters in children's books members of our class."

Laura Bush answers questions about the White House during a visit to Eden Park Elementary in Baton Rouge, Louisiana, on October 19, 2001.

Laura Bush

In 1969, Laura took a teaching job at John F. Kennedy Elementary School in Houston, Texas. While in Houston, she lived at the Chateaux Dijon apartment complex with her high school friend Jan O'Neill. Friends had told Laura it was a popular place for young, single people to live.

Laura had enjoyed teaching her second grade class so much that she asked to teach them again in the third grade. "I think people are truly called to teaching, and I loved every minute of it," she said years later. "Teaching is hard. It's hard to deal with a lot of personalities, you face a lot of challenges, but also it's very rewarding and it's never boring. I did think I was a good teacher. I think I'd be a lot better now."

As Laura spent more time in the classroom, she realized that she liked some parts of teaching better than others. She wasn't fond of math because she didn't think she was very good at it. But she thoroughly enjoyed reading to her students. That discovery led her down a new career path as a librarian. She moved to Austin and enrolled at the University of Texas to study library science. She graduated with a master's degree in library science in 1973.

After earning her master's degree, Laura returned to Houston. She took a job as the children's librarian at the McCrane-Kashmere Gardens Library. The library was part of the Houston public library system. A year later, Laura returned to Austin. There, she worked as a librarian at Dawson Elementary School. The job was ideal for Laura because it combined her childhood dream with what she had learned in college.

Laura had been in Austin for several years when her friend and former roommate Jan O'Neill urged her to meet a young man living in Midland. His name was George W. Bush. Laura resisted at first. "I thought he was someone who was interested in politics and that he would be someone I wouldn't be interested in because I was so uninterested in politics at the time." Finally she agreed to meet George at a barbecue at Jan's home.

During a visit to New York City on September 25, 2001, Laura Bush listens as students read letters they wrote to President Bush.

Whirlwind Romance

*L*aura recalled enjoying the company of the outgoing bachelor. "The thing I like about him was that he made me laugh," she told her mother afterward. As George and Laura talked, they discovered that they had attended the same junior high school, even though they didn't know each other then. They also realized they had lived in the same Houston apartment complex at the same time. The difference was that Laura had lived on the quiet side of Chateaux Dijon while George had lived on the loud side with all the parties.

Laura later was asked why she thought their friends arranged for her and George to meet. "Well," she said, "I guess it was because we were the only two people from that era in Midland who were still single."

*First Lady Laura Bush with
husband President George W. Bush.*

Laura Bush dances with her husband, President George W. Bush.

After their first meeting, they arranged a date to play miniature golf. From then on, George said he couldn't get the beautiful librarian with blue eyes and chestnut-colored hair off his mind. "There's something reassuring and calm, something beautiful about Laura that attracted me," he said.

Just days after they met, George had to leave for the Bush family's summer retreat in New England. Normally George enjoyed getting away to play golf and race speedboats. Now, he found himself anxious to get back to Texas.

He tried to call Laura. She rarely answered her phone, and when she did, she was usually too busy to talk for very long. Frustrated, George left the family retreat early and returned to Texas and Laura. For the next few weeks, he traveled to Austin nearly every weekend trying to win the heart of the quiet librarian. Three months after they met, Laura and George became engaged.

"I found her to be a very thoughtful, smart, interested person—one of the great listeners," George said of Laura. "And since I'm one of the big talkers, it was a great fit."

Laura's long-time friend Regan Gammon agreed. "We quickly realized that they were perfect complements to one another. Laura loved George's energy, and George loved the way she was so calm."

Mrs. Politician

*L*aura Welch and George W. Bush were married on November 5, 1977, in a small wedding at the First United Methodist Church in Midland. "I think it was a whirlwind romance because we were in our early thirties," she recalled. "I'm sure both of us thought, 'Gosh, we may never get married.' And we really wanted children. Plus, I lived in Austin and he lived in Midland; so if we were going to see each other all the time we needed to marry."

When they met, George W. Bush had been considering running for U.S. Congress. Following the wedding, the Bushes immediately began campaigning, making stops throughout west Texas. Suddenly, Laura Bush, who had been raised as a Democrat, was helping campaign for a Republican.

Upon getting married, Laura Bush quit her job and moved to Midland. Some people were surprised that she could leave her career behind so easily. For Bush, it wasn't a difficult decision. "I've always done what really traditional women do, and I've been very, very satisfied," she said.

Laura and George W. Bush's wedding. From left to right: Marvin, Dorothy, Neil, Columba, Jeb, Laura, George W., Barbara, George H.W., Dorothy.

In some ways, the big, boisterous Bush family was a dream come true for the shy librarian. "I like that part about marrying into the Bush family, having those brothers- and sisters-in-law," she said. "I always really wanted brothers and sisters." Likewise, the Bush family was thrilled to embrace its newest member. "Laura is a perfect match for George," said her mother-in-law, former First Lady Barbara Bush. "[She's a] catalyst in our family; she brings out the best in us."

Laura and George W. Bush

It was fortunate Laura Bush had such self-confidence. The reserved woman who hadn't cared much about politics was now the wife of a political candidate and had married into a political family. To calm her fears, her husband promised her she would never have to make any speeches.

However, three months later her husband had a scheduling conflict. He couldn't make an appearance he had arranged in Muleshoe, Texas. That left Laura Bush to stand on the courthouse steps and give a speech. "My husband told me I'd never have to make a political speech," she told the crowd that day. "So much for political promises." Flustered and unsure, she mumbled a few words about her husband's good qualities. Eventually she ran out of words and sat down. Her speech had lasted only a minute and a half.

Later during the campaign, the Bushes were driving home after a speech in Lubbock, Texas. George W. Bush asked his wife what she thought about his speech. She hesitated before replying. Once she had asked her mother-in-law for advice on being married to a politician. Barbara Bush had told her she should never criticize her husband's speeches. She decided to ignore her mother-in-law's advice for the moment and be honest. "Well," she said, "your speech wasn't very good." Her husband was so surprised that he drove their car right into the wall of their garage.

A Bush family photo. Top, left to right: Marvin, George, Jeb, George H.W., George W., Laura. Bottom, left to right: Columba, Noelle, Dorothy, Barbara, Neil.

President Ronald Reagan (left) and Vice President George H. W. Bush in 1981.

George W. Bush lost his bid for Congress, so the Bushes settled down to life in Midland. George W. Bush was running an independent gas and oil exploration company called Arbusto Energy, later renamed Bush Exploration. The Bushes also helped George's father, George H. W. Bush, when he ran for president during the 1980 election. George H. W. Bush was not chosen to be the Republican party's candidate, instead that honor went to Ronald Reagan. Reagan chose George H. W. Bush as his running mate. The two won the election, making George H. W. Bush the nation's new vice president.

Meanwhile, Laura and George W. Bush wanted to start a family. For three years, Laura Bush had tried to become pregnant. Finally, in the summer of 1981, she learned that she was going to have twins.

Close Call

*L*aura Bush's pregnancy was difficult. Doctors diagnosed her with toxemia. Toxemia can cause a pregnant woman to have blurred vision and high blood pressure, among other things. Even more frightening, the condition can lead to life-threatening seizures. These symptoms would require doctors to have to induce labor or perform a cesarean section to safely deliver the twins.

As the fall wore on, Bush's toxemia grew worse. In early November, she moved from Midland to Baylor Hospital in Dallas. She went into the hospital seven weeks before her due date. There, she was required to stay in bed all day. Two weeks later, doctors told her they couldn't wait any longer. Bush's kidneys were in danger of failing. They would have to deliver the twins by cesarean section.

Twins Jenna and Barbara Bush were born the morning of November 25, 1981. Jenna was named after Laura Bush's mother. Baby Jenna weighed just four pounds, twelve ounces. Barbara was named after George W. Bush's mother. Baby Barbara weighed five pounds, four ounces. Reporters soon arrived at the hospital. They wanted to get pictures of Vice President George H. W. Bush's new grandchildren.

George W. Bush holds his newborn twin daughters, Jenna and Barbara.

After the delivery, Laura Bush's health began to improve. Her husband was glad to see her feeling better, and he appreciated what she had gone through for their daughters. "She loves our daughters more than anything," he said. "She would lay her life down for them and nearly did at birth."

Laura Bush also remembered that her husband changed his share of diapers. "We brought home two little premature babies, and neither of us knew anything about babies. It was wild those first few weeks. But twins required both of us."

Another Campaign

*L*aura Bush was thrilled to be a mother at last. Raising her family in Midland, she was content to focus on her daughters and husband and leave the politics to the rest of the Bush family. In 1988, Laura and George W. Bush moved their young family to Washington, D.C., to help with George H. W. Bush's presidential campaign. The move gave Laura Bush a chance to grow closer to her mother-in-law, Barbara. The two remained close, vacationing together and even sharing favorite books. "She's a terrific role model for any woman… " Laura Bush said of her mother-in-law. "Very independent, very strong, irreverent and lots of fun."

George H. W. Bush won his presidential campaign. Soon after the election, Laura Bush and her family moved to Dallas, Texas. There, her husband and some other investors bought the Texas Rangers baseball team. It was a dream come true for George W. Bush. Soon after the purchase, he became the club's managing general partner.

Laura Bush

Laura Bush

Laura Bush, meanwhile, had her hands full raising twin girls. She still found time, however, to volunteer with several organizations, including the library at the elementary school where her daughters attended classes.

In the early 1990s, George W. Bush began talking about another political campaign. This time it was for the governor of Texas. Laura Bush was hesitant about her husband's goal. The family had just been through the heartbreak of George H. W. Bush's unsuccessful run for re-election as president. She worried that her husband's campaign would harm their daughters, who were almost teenagers. She also worried that the only reason he wanted to be governor was to carry on the Bush family legacy.

George W. Bush finally convinced his wife that he truly wanted to be governor, and she agreed to help him. She still disliked public speaking, but she did speak on his behalf to women's groups during his campaign. However, she made sure she had a script ready. "The idea of ad-libbing scared me to death," she said.

Laura Bush with her husband, Texas governor George W. Bush, in 1997.

For the Bushes, the 1994 Texas governor race was a tough fight. The incumbent Texas governor, Ann Richards, was popular. The Bushes knew it would be hard to defeat her. While campaigning, George W. Bush focused on what he wanted to do for Texas if elected. And he talked to his wife a lot. "We grew very close during the campaign because it was like we were in combat," he said later. He described himself and his wife as being "fellow warriors."

George W. Bush won the election and the Bush family moved into the governor's mansion in Austin. At first, Laura Bush wasn't sure she wanted to change her lifestyle to be the first lady of Texas. Her husband understood her feelings. He told her that if she didn't want to be a high-profile first lady, she didn't have to be. "You and the girls didn't ask to be put in this position," he told her. "And I promise I'm not going to make any of you do anything."

Laura Bush thought things over and made a decision. While she still wanted to help her daughters keep as much privacy as possible, she knew she couldn't be a first lady who no one ever saw. "I finally said, 'Well, if I'm going to be a public figure, I might as well do what I've always liked doing, which meant acting like a librarian and getting people interested in reading,'" she said. From that moment on, Laura Bush had a cause.

Fabulous First Lady

*A*s the first lady of Texas, Laura Bush organized the first-ever Texas Book Festival in 1996. She personally invited more than 100 Texas writers to read at the opening event. Then she traveled around the state to bring attention to the issue of illiteracy. Wherever she went, she encouraged people to read. She challenged local leaders to create and improve reading programs. Thanks to her efforts, Texans raised $900,000 to buy books for the state's libraries.

Gone was the shy woman who had given the short, awkward political speech in Muleshoe, Texas. Laura Bush was now poised, confident, and articulate. She spoke about literacy at the Republican National Convention in 1996. After her polished speech, her husband simply stared at her in awe. "You have to remember that this was a woman who used to think a good speech was putting her finger to her mouth in a school library and telling her students, 'Shhhh,'" Governor Bush joked. "To me, it has been remarkable… to watch what has happened to her."

Laura Bush

Laura Bush hands out books to students at the National Book Festival at the Library of Congress.

In 1997, Laura Bush became involved in the Reach Out and Read program. The program seeks to make literacy a standard part of pediatric care. In this program, pediatricians encourage parents to read aloud to their young children. Pediatricians also give books to patients when they come in for visits. By doing this, young children should be more prepared for school.

Laura Bush persuaded her mother-in-law, Barbara Bush, to help in her community literacy work, as well. As the first lady of the United States, Barbara Bush had started a foundation for family literacy. That foundation helped Laura Bush start the First Lady's Family Literacy Initiative for Texas. It awarded literacy grants to nonprofit groups.

Along with promoting programs to encourage reading, the first lady of Texas volunteered her time and her high-profile position to assist child protection workers. She provided support and resources to help them care for abused children throughout the state. She also served on several library and reading-related advisory councils. And, she helped raise money to support the arts and breast cancer research. Quietly and while maintaining her privacy, Laura Bush became one of the most effective first ladies in the history of Texas.

Laura and George W. Bush's twin daughters, Barbara (left) and Jenna, at a political rally in Austin, Texas, on March 7, 2000.

Despite her many activities, Bush maintained her family as a top priority. "Even if I'm traveling all over the state, I'll get home by four, which is right before the children get out of school," she said. "We do very few big night events, and we're at home on the weekends." The governor's mansion also took on the look of any home inhabited by teenagers. Barbara and Jenna often had friends over for snacking and studying.

Bush's commitment to leading as normal a life as possible was evident in many ways. In an interview, Bush recounted an occasion when she and the twins visited a well-known discount store near their lake home in Athens, Texas. At the time, Bush was the first lady of Texas. She was waiting in the checkout line with Barbara and Jenna when another shopper asked her, "Don't I know you?"

"I'm Laura Bush," she answered. "Sorry, that doesn't ring a bell," the other shopper said. Bush recalled that as soon as they left the store, she and her daughters burst out laughing.

In 1995, Laura Bush was saddened by the death of her father, Harold. He died at age 82 after developing Alzheimer's disease. She recalled how he had loved to laugh and joke, and she noted how her husband reminded her of her father in that way.

White House Bound

*G*eorge W. Bush easily won re-election as Texas governor in 1998. His popularity put him in the national spotlight. Republican party leaders began talking about him running for president in 2000.

As before when he talked about running for governor, Laura Bush was concerned. She didn't want the spotlight of a presidential campaign to harm their daughters. She also remembered how hard it was to hear people say unkind things about her father-in-law, former President George H. W. Bush, during his unsuccessful campaign in 1992. "It's very difficult to read criticism of someone you love," she said. She feared people would be saying things about her husband that she knew weren't true.

Laura Bush wanted to know if her husband genuinely wanted the president's job. When George W. Bush decided that he truly did want to run for president, she took the news in stride. She quietly vowed not to let the campaign drive her, her husband, or her family crazy.

Laura Bush at a campaign rally in support of her husband, Texas governor George W. Bush, in Bangor, Maine, March 3, 2000.

"The campaign is anxiety-provoking, there's no doubt about it," she said. "What I remember from the '92 election is waking up every morning and feeling anxious when George went out to get the newspaper. I'd think, 'What's it going to be today?' I'm certainly aware that we could get to that, but this time it's easier to slough off. I think when it's your parents, it's harder, just like it would be if it were your child."

Throughout the campaign, Laura Bush continued to keep a low profile. She worked hard to keep the lives of her daughters private, as well. She visited schools and talked about education, which was one of the key issues her husband was focusing on. She also gave more speeches.

Despite Laura Bush's preference to be in the background, reporters fired questions at her during the campaign, too. One reporter asked which former first lady she'd be more like, Hillary Rodham Clinton or Barbara Bush. She replied, "I think I'll just be Laura Bush." George W. Bush echoed his wife's individuality. When campaigning, he liked to boast about her. "The best decision I ever made was to ask Laura to marry me," he said.

Also during the campaign, a newspaper published a report about the car accident that Laura Bush had been involved in at age 17. "It was hard to have that come out," she told a reporter. "Although I expected it to come out… It was certainly no secret. All of my friends knew, everyone in Midland knew. But that's hard…"

While on the road, Laura Bush campaigned. While at home, she kept her family calm and close. "We have a life, friends and family outside politics," she said. "We'll stay the same people, no matter what happens."

Laura Bush

The Adventure Begins

*T*he 2000 election was indeed an adventure. The vote was so close that it took weeks to declare a winner. The Bush family was especially tense during this time. Laura Bush did her best to keep everyone calm.

"The best evidence of that is the way she conducted herself during those awful 35 days when the election was up in the air," said former President George H. W. Bush. "It was a savage, horrible period. But she never got rattled, never got vindictive." Her reputation as a true lady had grown even stronger.

When her husband was finally declared the winner, Laura Bush began making plans to move to Washington, D.C. It was an incredibly busy time. The Bushes were just finishing construction of their new ranch home in Crawford, Texas. She had been very involved in the building project. Now she had to coordinate a move to Washington, D.C., as well.

Laura Bush also had to field even more questions from reporters. They loved to ask her what role she saw for herself as first lady. "I actually think that the role is whatever the first lady wants it to be," she told them a few months into her husband's term.

"First ladies have worked on issues that they were already interested in, and that's what I'm doing. Education is what I know about, and teaching is what's important to me. I think the American people think that the first lady ought to get to do whatever she wants to do."

George W. Bush embraces his wife, Laura, after his acceptance speech at the Republican National Convention in Philadelphia, Pennsylvania, on August 3, 2000.

New First Lady

*T*he position of the first lady has been as different as the women who have held it. Some first ladies, such as Bess Truman, kept a low profile while in the White House. Other first ladies, such as Eleanor Roosevelt and Hillary Rodham Clinton, chose to be very active.

Laura Bush made no secret of the fact that she wanted her time as first lady to be quiet and traditional. When asked what she would do as first lady, she replied, "What really traditional women do." Since she had never been that interested in politics, she hoped to keep her life as normal as possible. She also said she didn't intend to influence her husband's beliefs. Once a reporter asked her if she disagreed with her husband on several controversial issues. She replied, "If I differ with my husband, I'm not going to tell you."

During her first six months in Washington, D.C., Laura Bush moved the offices of the first lady. They had been in the political West Wing of the White House. She moved them to the more traditional East Wing. When she advised her husband, it was always in private.

President George W. Bush and First Lady Laura Bush

President Bush and First Lady Laura Bush walk out of the Rose Garden to the South Lawn of the White House.

She continued to work quietly on causes related to reading and literacy. One of them was promoting the Ready to Read, Ready to Learn initiative. She spoke out about the need to recruit more teachers, too.

Bush caused a stir when she disappeared for several weeks shortly after her husband became president. Rumors swirled about where she might have gone. As it turned out, she was out shopping for linens and furniture for their new ranch home in Crawford, Texas. She felt it was important to get the new house prepared so it could serve as a retreat for the family. She was also practical enough to know that the presidency doesn't last forever. Eventually, the Bush family would need their own place to call home.

Laura Bush was different from the woman who preceded her, former First Lady Hillary Rodham Clinton. She also appeared to be very popular. A poll in summer of 2001 showed Laura Bush had a 64 percent approval rating among Americans. That was an even higher rating than her husband had at the time!

Comforter In Chief

*L*ike her husband, Laura Bush found that her role changed after the terrorist attacks of September 11, 2001. On that day, she was on her way to meet with Senator Edward Kennedy for a Senate Education Committee briefing when she learned of the attacks. "I remember thinking that nothing ever would be the same," she said.

The first lady interrupted her work on education and literacy issues to help the nation cope with the attacks. In public statements, she urged parents to keep a close eye on their children. She also encouraged parents to make sure their children felt safe in their homes and schools. She spent even more time than usual visiting schools and talking about the tragedy with students.

In early October, the first lady visited New York City. She stopped at a fire station that had lost half of its firefighters. She left a bouquet of flowers tied with a red, white, and blue ribbon. She also wrote a note in the fire station's journal. "To the firefighters of Battalion 9," she wrote, "you showed the world that

Laura and President George W. Bush

honor and bravery are alive in New York City. Thank you for being heroes. God bless you, Laura Bush."

Next, she stopped at New York Public School 41. The school had nearly doubled in size after accepting students misplaced by the World Trade Center attacks. At the school, one student asked, "How do you get to be president?" The first lady smiled and told her she just married one.

As the war on terrorism wore on, Laura Bush remained in the spotlight. On November 17, 2001, she became the first first lady ever to give the weekly presidential radio address. In her address, she spoke out against the treatment of women and children under Afghanistan's brutal Taliban government.

Reporters began calling the first lady the Comforter in Chief. The title matched her husband's role as Commander in Chief. It was a role that suited her well.

A Normal Life

"*J*ust like I supposedly calm him down, he adds a lot of excitement to my life," the first lady said of her husband. President George W. Bush added, "Politics doesn't totally consume her, and as a result, it doesn't totally consume me."

As their time in the White House continues, it seems likely that the first lady will keep their family life as normal as possible. "We find a lot of refuge in each other… " she said of her relationship with her husband. That helps them weather whatever crisis may come along.

It also helps that Laura Bush shares her husband's well-known sense of humor. She's not above putting her husband in his place at times. A mutual friend said that the first lady has been known to tell the president to "Rein it in, Bubba."

Laura Bush confirms that. "We do tease each other," she said. "We've had a million nicknames for each other—ridiculous names. Our latest is Bushie," she adds in a sweet, Texas drawl.

President Bush and First Lady Laura Bush at a White House reception.

President George W. Bush and First Lady Laura Bush wave before boarding Air Force One.

"We talk about issues, we talk about personalities," she said. "But we also spend a lot of time talking about what every other couple talks about: our children."

When not on official business, the first lady enjoys reading, gardening, and spending time with her family. The Bushes also love to relax at their new ranch home. While there, the first lady likes to cook Tex-Mex food, and the president likes to fish. In between duties, Laura Bush enjoys vacationing with childhood friends. She has taken river-rafting trips in the Grand Canyon and gone bird-watching in Belize.

Shortly after moving to the White House, Laura Bush invited several of her friends and members of the Austin Garden Club to visit. One night they changed into their pajamas and stayed up late talking in the White House solarium. Despite the pressures and responsibilities of being first lady, Laura Bush was still simply being Laura Bush.

Timeline

November 4, 1946: Laura Welch is born in Midland, Texas.

1963: Laura Welch is involved in fatal car accident.

1968: Laura Welch graduates from Southern Methodist University.

1973: Laura Welch graduates from the University of Texas at Austin and begins working as a children's librarian.

1977: Laura Welch marries George W. Bush.

1981: Laura Bush gives birth to twin daughters, Jenna and Barbara.

1994: George W. Bush is elected governor of Texas, making Laura Bush first lady of the state.

1996: Laura Bush organizes the first-ever Texas Book Festival.

2000: George W. Bush is elected president of the United States, and Laura Bush becomes the first lady of the United States.

2001: Terrorists attack the U.S. Laura Bush gives speeches to help the nation deal with the attacks.

Web Sites

Would you like to learn more about Laura Bush? Please visit **www.abdopub.com** to find up-to-date Web site links about Laura Bush and her husband, President George W. Bush. These links are routinely monitored and updated to provide the most current information available.

Laura Bush

Glossary

Alzheimer's disease

A brain disorder that causes memory loss and changes in personality.

articulate

Able to express one's self clearly and effectively.

boisterous

High spirited, noisy, or rowdy.

cesarean section

The delivery of a baby through surgery when a normal delivery is too dangerous.

Democratic Party

A political party that believes in social change and strong government.

illiteracy

An inability to read or write.

incumbent

A person who holds a political office.

initiative

The procedure by which a new law is enacted.

introvert

A shy or reserved person.

literacy

The ability to read and write.

matriarch

The woman who is the head of her family.

pediatrician

A doctor who cares for children.

Republican National Convention

A national meeting held every four years during which the Republican Party chooses its candidates for president and vice president.

Republican Party

A political party that is conservative and believes in small government.

solarium

A glass-enclosed porch or room.

Index